Dancing Games: 50 Fun & Interactive Movement Games for Children.

Dance is a universal language that transcends barriers, bringing joy and creative expression to all ages. This book, "Dancing games," is designed for educators, dance instructors, and caregivers who wish to introduce movement and dance to children aged 4 to 12 in a playful, educational manner. These carefully curated dance games emphasize creativity, cooperation, self-expression, and physical development, making dance accessible to every child.

The games in this book are categorized into warm-ups, icebreakers, memory games, body coordination, group coordination, space management, rhythm sense, stamina building, expression and emotions, and storytelling. Minimal props are needed, and each game has been thoughtfully designed to suit classroom settings. Let's dive into this world of dance and watch young dancers thrive! Teachers can personalize each activity to suit their preferred dance style. Additionally, teachers can create their own worksheets to adapt and expand the activities creatively.

About the author:

Ms. C.R. Lakshmi Karthik is a classical dancer and educator practicing Bharathanatyam & kathak. She is holding a Masters in Bharathanatyam & an Advanced Diploma in Kathak. She is dance research scholar who works with dance intervention & other perspectives of learning dance. With an intention to promoting classical dance, she established the Sri Nrithya Lakshana Dance School in Bangalore. The institution focuses on imparting traditional techniques while encouraging innovation and individual expression. Sri Nrithya Lakshana's teaching philosophy blends traditional techniques with innovative methods, making dance engaging and enjoyable. By incorporating dance games and interactive activities, the institute redefined classical dance education. Despite initial criticism from others, Lakshmi Karthik remained steadfast in her vision and nurtured students into skilled performers. Under her guidance, many students have gained proficiency in dance, contributing to the cultural integrity of India.

Contents

1. WARM UPS

1.1 Mirror Movements

Objective:

To improve focus, body awareness, and coordination while encouraging collaboration and empathy.

Procedure:

- Pair up the children and assign one as the leader and the other as the "mirror."

- The leader performs simple dance moves (like arm waves, head tilts, or leg lifts) while the "mirror" copies them as closely as possible.

- Switch roles after a minute or two.

- To increase the challenge, use more complex or faster movements.

Outcome:

Children develop better body control, attentiveness, and the ability to work in partnership while experiencing the perspective of both leader and follower.

1.2 Follow the Leader

Objective:

To enhance listening skills, imitation, and the ability to follow sequences while having fun.

Procedure:

- The teacher starts as the leader, demonstrating simple movements like marching, jumping, or clapping.

- Children follow and imitate the leader's movements.

- Gradually increase the complexity of the movements or add music for a rhythmic challenge.

- Allow children to take turns leading the group.

Outcome:

Children learn to focus, improve memory, and gain confidence in leading and following, fostering a sense of unity and participation.

1.3 Stretch and Shake

Objective:

To prepare the body for movement, increase flexibility, and release tension in a playful way.

Procedure:

- Begin with gentle stretching from head to toe — neck rolls, shoulder shrugs, toe touches, etc.

- Transition to a "shake-off" where children shake different body parts — arms, legs, hips, and head.

- Encourage children to shake creatively to the rhythm of the music.

Outcome:

Children become more aware of their bodies, improve flexibility, and release energy positively, reducing anxiety and boosting readiness for activity.

1.4 Shape Dance

Objective:

To stimulate imagination, spatial awareness, and creativity while reinforcing the understanding of basic shapes.

Procedure:

- Call out a shape (circle, square, triangle) and challenge children to create it using their bodies individually or in small groups.

- As they get comfortable, encourage them to add movement — for example, spinning in a circle or forming a square with walking steps.

- Integrate music to maintain energy and engagement.

Outcome:

Children enhance their ability to visualize and create shapes, improve spatial reasoning, and engage creatively through physical expression.

1.5 Flash Card Freeze

Objective:

To enhance quick thinking, creativity, and body part recognition while maintaining focus.

Procedure:

- Show a flashcard displaying a body part (like "arm," "leg," "head").

- When the card is shown, children creatively move the specified body part — they might wiggle, wave, or shake it.

- Occasionally shout "Freeze!" and observe their poses for fun.

- Increase the challenge by showing two or more flashcards at once.

Outcome:

Children strengthen their knowledge of body parts, improve coordination, and practice quick decision-making in a playful environment.

2. ICE BREAKERS:

2.1 Dance Name Game

Objective:

To help children learn each other's names, build confidence, and encourage creative self-expression.

Procedure:

- Children form a circle.

- One child step into the centre, says their name rhythmically (like "My name is Mia!" with a clap or stomp) and adds a simple dance move.

- The group repeats the name and move together.

- Continue until everyone has had a turn.

- If the group is large, divide them into smaller circles to maintain engagement.

Outcome:

Children become more comfortable with each other, develop rhythm and coordination, and strengthen memory by associating names with movements.

2.2 Move and Greet

Objective:

To promote social interaction, active listening, and creative movement in a relaxed, playful atmosphere.

Procedure:

- Play upbeat music and have children dance freely around the room.

- When the music stops, call out a greeting style — like a wave, twirl, or shake.

- Children find a partner, introduce themselves, and greet each other using the specified dance move.

- Repeat a few rounds, encouraging them to greet a new person each time.

Outcome:

Children gain confidence in meeting new people, enhance their social skills, and creatively express themselves through movement.

2.3 Dance Like...

Objective:
To spark imagination, increase body awareness, and build confidence through expressive movement.

Procedure:

- Call out an animal (like a bird, elephant) or an object (like a robot, balloon).

- Children use their bodies to interpret the prompt through dance — flapping like a bird, stomping like an elephant, etc.

- Encourage everyone to move freely and creatively, and praise unique interpretations.

- Optionally, ask children to guess what others are dancing like.

Outcome:
Children expand their creative thinking, develop their gross motor skills, and become more comfortable exploring various movement styles.

2.4 Rhythm Circle

Objective:

To enhance group coordination, rhythm awareness, and creativity while encouraging collaboration.

Procedure:

- Children stand in a circle.

- The first person creates a simple dance move to a rhythm (like a stomp-clap-spin).

- The next person repeats the move and adds their own, passing the sequence along.

- Continue until the sequence reaches the end of the circle.

- If the sequence becomes too complex, start a new one.

Outcome:

Children strengthen their memory, rhythm skills, and teamwork, while appreciating the creativity of their peers.

2.5 Freeze Dance with Props

Objective:
To develop body control, focus, and creative use of space while boosting confidence.

Procedure:

- Give each child a scarf or ribbon.

- Play music and let children dance freely with their props.

- When the music stops, they must "freeze" in a creative pose, holding the prop in a unique way.

- Encourage them to think of new poses each time the music pauses.

Outcome:
Children improve their ability to control their bodies, make quick decisions, and explore creative uses of props in movement.

3. MEMORY GAMES:

3.1 Copycat Chain

Objective:

To enhance memory, concentration, and sequencing skills while encouraging creativity and teamwork.

Procedure:

- Arrange children in a line.

- The first child performs a simple dance move (like a clap, jump, or spin).

- The second child copies the first move and adds their own.

- The process continues, with each child copying the entire sequence before adding their move.

- If a mistake is made, start over or continue with encouragement.

Outcome:

Children develop the ability to recall and replicate sequences while boosting their confidence, coordination, and cooperation with peers.

3.2 Recall and Dance

Objective:

To strengthen short-term memory, focus, and the ability to translate visual input into physical movement.

Procedure:

- Show a series of flashcards with illustrated dance moves (like a stomp, twirl, or wave).

- Allow a few seconds for children to memorize the sequence.

- Hide the flashcards and ask the children to perform the sequence from memory.

- Gradually increase the complexity of the sequences as they progress.

Outcome:

Children improve their memory recall and motor planning, along with developing better attention to detail and observation skills.

3.3 What Changed?

Objective:

To enhance observation, adaptability, and memory through quick thinking.

Procedure:

- Establish a simple dance pattern (e.g., step-touch-clap).

- Have children dance to the pattern several times.

- Secretly change one part of the pattern (e.g., replace a clap with a jump).

- Ask children to identify the change and adapt to the new pattern.

Outcome:

Children strengthen their observation skills, adaptability, and quick decision-making, fostering awareness of details and flexibility.

3.4 Dance Recall

Objective:

To boost memory retention, sequencing skills, and confidence in performing learned material.

Procedure:

- Teach a brief, structured dance sequence with clear, simple moves.

- Repeat the sequence a few times for reinforcement.

- Pause the music and challenge the children to perform the sequence without guidance.

- Gradually increase the complexity or length of the sequence.

Outcome:

Children enhance their ability to recall and reproduce movements, building confidence in performing from memory while reinforcing sequencing skills.

3.5 Step Sequence

Objective:
To develop pattern recognition, memory expansion, and creative thinking.

Procedure:

- Start with a simple step pattern (e.g., step-clap-hop).

- Ask children to memorize and repeat the pattern.

- Gradually expand the sequence by adding additional steps (e.g., step-clap-hop-turn).

- Challenge children to create and add their own steps to the sequence.

Outcome:
Children strengthen their working memory, ability to recognize and create patterns, and engage creatively in a group setting.

4. BODY COORDINATION:

4.1 Step and Slide

Objective:

To develop coordination, spatial awareness, and rhythm while encouraging focus and creativity.

Procedure:

- Have children stand in a designated space.

- Teach them to step to the side and slide their feet together, alternating directions.

- Add claps, snaps, or stomps for extra challenge and rhythmic complexity.

- Encourage variations like forward-backward slides or diagonal movements.

Outcome:

Children improve coordination, balance, and rhythm while exploring dynamic movement. They also gain confidence in moving within a shared space.

4.2 Cross the Midline

Objective:

To enhance brain-body connection, coordination, and cognitive flexibility by crossing the body's midline.

Procedure:

- Have children stand in place.

- Guide them to touch their right hand to their left knee and then their left hand to their right knee, alternating continuously.

- Gradually increase the speed for a greater challenge.

- Add rhythmic claps or background music for extra stimulation.

Outcome:

Children strengthen their ability to coordinate both sides of the body, which supports cognitive development and motor planning. They also enhance focus and self-regulation.

4.3 Balancing Act

Objective:

To develop balance, body control, and core strength while encouraging creativity in movement.

Procedure:

- Ask children to balance on one leg and try simple movements like knee lifts or slow kicks.

- Challenge them to create dance moves that maintain balance, like slow spins or tilts.

- Have them switch legs periodically to balance both sides.

- Add a creative element by asking them to imagine they are balancing on a narrow beam or a swaying boat.

Outcome:

Children build core strength, balance, and coordination while increasing their focus and self-awareness. They also learn to control their movements with intention.

4.4 Hand-Foot Tap

Objective:

To boost coordination, memory, and rhythm through patterned movement.

Procedure:

- Teach a simple pattern like tapping right hand to left foot, left hand to right foot, then clap.

- Gradually increase the speed while keeping accuracy.

- Create variations like adding a hop or switching the pattern sequence.

- Encourage children to create their own patterns to share with the group.

Outcome:

Children enhance coordination, memory, and the ability to perform sequences. They also gain confidence in creating and sharing their own movement patterns.

4.5 Body Isolation Dance

Objective:

To increase body awareness, control, and creativity by focusing on isolating specific body parts.

Procedure:

- Ask children to focus on moving only one part of their body, such as just their shoulders, hips, or head.

- Demonstrate isolated movements like shoulder shrugs, hip rolls, or head tilts.

- Encourage creative combinations — moving shoulders in one direction while hips move in another.

- Challenge them to create short dance sequences using isolated movements.

Outcome:

Children improve their control over specific body parts, become more aware of their bodies, and develop creativity in movement. It also helps them connect movement to music more expressively.

5. GROUP COORDINATION:

5.1 Dance Together

Objective:

To encourage teamwork, creativity, and coordination by creating synchronized group movements.

Procedure:

- Divide children into small groups of 3 to 4.

- Challenge each group to create a simple, synchronized dance move or short sequence.

- Allow time for practice, focusing on timing and coordination.

- Have each group share their sequence with the class. Optionally, combine groups to create a larger synchronized performance.

Outcome:

Children develop collaboration skills, creativity, and the ability to coordinate movements with others. They also gain confidence in performing for an audience.

5.2 Circle Groove

Objective:
To build rhythmic awareness, focus, and cooperative skills while exploring group dynamics.

Procedure:

- Form a circle with all children.

- The first person performs a dance move, and the next person copies it while adding their own.

- The pattern continues around the circle, with each child replicating and adding a new move.

- Change the tempo periodically — slow, medium, fast — to challenge timing and adaptability.

Outcome:
Children enhance their ability to imitate and adapt to others' movements, build focus, and strengthen group cohesion through shared movement.

5.3 Partner Pulse

Objective:

To strengthen cooperation, listening skills, and rhythmic coordination between partners.

Procedure:

- Pair up children and have them face each other.

- Instruct them to create a simple rhythmic dance that mirrors or complements each other's movements — like clapping, stepping, or swaying in sync.

- Encourage them to maintain eye contact and communicate non-verbally to stay synchronized.

- Allow time for partners to share their routines with the class.

Outcome:

Children learn to work closely with a partner, improving coordination, non-verbal communication, and rhythmic awareness. They also build trust and collaboration skills.

5.4 Connected Movement

Objective:

To develop teamwork, trust, and spatial awareness while exploring movement as a connected unit.

Procedure:

- Have children hold hands in pairs or small groups.

- Guide them through movements like swaying, spinning, stepping, or shifting levels (high, medium, low) while remaining connected.

- Challenge them to create sequences that incorporate synchronized or complementary movements.

- Experiment with creating shapes or traveling through space while maintaining connection.

Outcome:

Children increase their sense of spatial awareness, build trust within the group, and explore cooperative movement while creatively expressing themselves.

5.5 Flash Card Relay

Objective:
To build quick thinking, teamwork, and dynamic movement skills through fast-paced group interaction.

Procedure:

- Divide children into small groups.

- Show a flashcard with a movement prompt (e.g., "jump," "spin," "wave").

- The first group quickly performs the movement and then "passes" the prompt to the next group.

- Continue until all groups have performed. Increase the challenge by combining multiple flashcards for sequential movements.

Outcome:
Children practice quick decision-making, enhance group coordination, and improve their ability to respond to visual cues while staying engaged.

6. SPACE MANAGEMENT:

6.1 Bubble Dance

Objective:

To help children understand and respect personal space while developing spatial awareness and creative movement.

Procedure:

- Ask children to imagine they are inside an invisible bubble that they should protect.

- Play music and encourage them to dance freely while keeping their "bubble" intact.

- If they accidentally "pop" someone else's bubble by touching them, gently remind them to be mindful of space.

- Add challenges like varying speeds or levels (high, medium, low) to increase difficulty.

Outcome:

Children learn to navigate shared spaces respectfully, enhance body control, and build spatial awareness while enjoying creative movement.

6.2 Spot Dance

Objective:

To develop body control, self-regulation, and the ability to express creatively within boundaries.

Procedure:

- Mark small areas or spots for each child to dance within. These can be made with floor markers, cones, or taped sections.

- Play music and encourage them to dance freely while staying within their designated spot.

- Challenge them to use all available space — exploring high, low, fast, and slow movements.

- Occasionally instruct them to change spots without "popping" others' bubbles.

Outcome:

Children improve their ability to control movement within confined spaces, respect boundaries, and expand their creativity within limits.

6.3 Traveling Pathways

Objective:

To develop spatial awareness, motor planning, and creativity while understanding movement pathways.

Procedure:

- Demonstrate moving through space using different pathways like zig-zags, circles, straight lines, and curves.

- Ask children to explore these pathways while traveling across the room, adjusting speed and direction.

- Ensure they maintain awareness of others to avoid collisions.

- Add variations like hopping in zig-zags or spinning in circles for complexity.

Outcome:

Children enhance their ability to navigate space, adapt their movements, and maintain awareness of others while developing creative movement skills.

6.4 Personal Space Challenge

Objective:

To promote spatial awareness, impulse control, and coordination while encouraging respect for personal space.

Procedure:

- Gather children in a limited space and encourage them to dance freely.

- The goal is to move creatively without touching or bumping into anyone else.

- Occasionally shrink the space or increase the number of participants to challenge their ability to adapt.

- Discuss the importance of awareness and respecting boundaries afterward.

Outcome:

Children learn to control their bodies in crowded spaces, develop better awareness of their surroundings, and practice self-regulation while moving creatively.

6.5 Flash Card Directions

Objective:

To improve directional understanding, following instructions, and spatial orientation while fostering quick thinking.

Procedure:

- Prepare flashcards with directional prompts like forward, backward, left, right, up, and down.

- Show a flashcard, and children must quickly adjust their movement to match the direction.

- Combine directions for complexity, like "Forward and left!" or "Backward and down!"

- Play music to keep energy levels high and pause occasionally for quick directions.

Outcome:

Children sharpen their understanding of directions, enhance their ability to follow instructions quickly, and develop adaptability in movement.

7. RHYTHM SENSE:

7.1 Clap and Tap

Objective:
To develop rhythm, coordination, and the ability to synchronize movements with auditory cues.

Procedure:

- The teacher demonstrates a series of rhythmic claps (e.g., clap-clap-tap, clap-tap-clap).

- Children repeat the pattern, adding dance moves like stomps, jumps, or spins.

- Gradually increase complexity by adding pauses, faster rhythms, or alternating between claps and taps.

- Allow children to create and share their own rhythmic patterns with the group.

Outcome:
Children enhance their sense of rhythm, coordination, and listening skills while building confidence in leading and following movement patterns.

7.2 Beat and Bounce

Objective:

To build body control, musicality, and creative movement through responding to rhythmic beats.

Procedure:

- Play a drumbeat or rhythmic music with a clear, steady tempo.

- Children bounce to the beat with different body parts — knees, hips, or whole-body bounces.

- Encourage them to add creative movements like arm waves, spins, or hops while maintaining the bounce.

- Occasionally pause the beat and challenge them to freeze in a creative pose.

Outcome:

Children strengthen their connection to rhythm, explore creative expression, and improve balance and coordination.

7.3 Step to the Beat

Objective:

To develop timing, coordination, and rhythmic awareness while reinforcing steady beat recognition.

Procedure:

- Play rhythmic music with a clear, steady beat.

- Guide children to march, stomp, or step in time with the beat, adjusting their movements to match the tempo.

- Gradually vary the speed of the music — slow, medium, fast — and observe their adaptability.

- Encourage them to add hand claps, arm swings, or vocal sounds to enrich the experience.

Outcome:

Children improve their ability to synchronize movements to music, develop rhythmic accuracy, and enhance focus and body coordination.

7.4 Rhythmic Imitation

Objective:

To enhance auditory discrimination, imitation skills, and creative movement through rhythmic patterning.

Procedure:

- Create a simple rhythmic pattern using body percussion like claps, snaps, or stomps.

- Children imitate the pattern with both sound and matching dance moves.

- Increase complexity by layering more sounds or changing the tempo.

- Allow children to take turns creating patterns for the group to imitate.

Outcome:

Children develop their memory, listening skills, and ability to translate sound into movement, fostering creativity and collaboration.

7.5 Flash Card Rhythms

Objective:

To reinforce rhythm recognition, quick thinking, and creative movement through visual cues.

Procedure:

- Create flashcards displaying rhythmic patterns using symbols (like quarter notes, eighth notes) or simple dot patterns.

- Show a flashcard and ask children to interpret the rhythm with movements — like jumps, claps, or stomps.

- Allow them to create their own rhythmic movements based on the visual cues.

- Gradually increase complexity with combined flashcards showing multiple rhythms.

Outcome:

Children build rhythm literacy, learn to connect visual and auditory information, and expand their movement creativity.

8. STAMINA BUILDING:

8.1 Fast and Slow

Objective:

To develop endurance, control, and adaptability while exploring contrasting movement qualities.

Procedure:

- Play music that alternates between fast and slow tempos, or switch between upbeat and mellow tracks.

- Encourage children to dance energetically during fast sections and smoothly during slow sections.

- Gradually make transitions quicker to challenge their adaptability.

- Explore contrasting movements like fast jumps and slow stretches, quick spins and gentle sways.

Outcome:

Children enhance their cardiovascular endurance, body control, and ability to adapt quickly to changing tempos. They also build awareness of musical dynamics.

8.2 Jump and Groove

Objective:

To build stamina, coordination, and rhythm through dynamic jumping movements.

Procedure:

- Play upbeat music with a strong, steady beat.

- Guide children through jumping sequences like jumping jacks, side-to-side hops, or criss-cross jumps.

- Add rhythmic movements between jumps — like claps, hip sways, or arm rolls — to maintain engagement.

- Create a playful challenge by calling out different jump variations or having children lead the sequence.

Outcome:

Children increase their endurance, strengthen coordination, and develop rhythmic consistency while having fun.

8.3 Run and Dance

Objective:

To build cardiovascular endurance, creativity, and quick transitions between running and dancing.

Procedure:

- Set up a safe space for short runs (like from one end of the room to the other).

- Children run quickly for a few seconds, then stop and perform an expressive dance move or a short sequence.

- Repeat several times, varying the dance moves — like spins, leaps, or creative poses.

- Incorporate playful prompts like "run like a cheetah, dance like a peacock" for added creativity.

Outcome:

Children develop cardiovascular fitness, agility, and creativity while learning to transition smoothly between dynamic and controlled movements.

8.4 Speed Challenge

Objective:

To enhance speed, coordination, and focus through quick, energetic dance sequences.

Procedure:

- Play high-energy music with a fast tempo.

- Challenge children to dance as fast as they can while maintaining control — think fast footwork, rapid arm movements, or quick spins.

- Alternate between short bursts of fast dancing and brief rest periods.

- Create team challenges, like mirroring a partner's fast moves or competing to maintain the rhythm without mistakes.

Outcome:

Children improve their stamina, quick thinking, and ability to maintain coordination during fast-paced movement. They also practice managing energy effectively.

8.5 Flash Card Circuit

Objective:
To build endurance, quick reaction time, and dynamic movement skills using visual cues.

Procedure:

- Prepare flashcards with energetic actions like "jump," "spin," "kick," "skip," or "run."

- Show a flashcard, and children perform the corresponding movement quickly and energetically.

- Create sequences by showing multiple flashcards in a row to create a mini circuit.

- Gradually increase the speed and complexity of the sequence for a greater challenge.

Outcome:
Children develop physical endurance, quick response abilities, and learn to follow visual cues while expanding their movement vocabulary.

9. EXPRESSION AND EMOTIONS:

9.1 Emotion Dance

Objective:

To explore emotional expression through movement, enhancing empathy, creativity, and self-awareness.

Procedure:

- Discuss different emotions — happy, sad, angry, surprised — and what they might look like in dance.

- Play a variety of music that evokes different emotions and ask children to move in a way that expresses the feeling.

- Call out an emotion and encourage them to adjust their movements to reflect it.

- Invite children to share and discuss how they expressed each emotion.

Outcome:

Children gain confidence in expressing their emotions through movement, develop empathy by understanding others' feelings, and explore creative self-expression.

9.2 Character Dance

Objective:

To enhance imagination, storytelling, and expressive movement by embodying characters.

Procedure:

- Choose familiar characters from stories, movies, or cartoons.

- Describe each character's personality traits and emotions, discussing how they might move.

- Play music that suits the character, and encourage children to dance as if they are that character.

- Optionally, have them interact with others "in character" to add depth to their expression.

Outcome:

Children build their ability to express personality through movement, expand their imagination, and develop narrative thinking by embodying different roles.

9.3 Freeze and Face

Objective:

To develop self-control, focus, and the ability to express emotions physically and facially.

Procedure:

- Play lively music and let children dance freely.

- Pause the music and call out an emotion (like "excited" or "frustrated").

- Children freeze in a pose that expresses the emotion while also using facial expressions.

- Discuss how they used their body and face to convey the feeling.

Outcome:

Children improve their ability to control their movements, interpret emotions physically, and use facial expressions to deepen their emotional expression.

9.4 Mirror Emotions

Objective:

To develop empathy, observation skills, and the ability to communicate emotions non-verbally.

Procedure:

- Pair children up and designate one as the "leader" and the other as the "mirror."

- The leader expresses a dance movement that reflects a specific emotion, while the mirror copies as accurately as possible.

- Switch roles so each child experiences leading and following.

- Discuss how it felt to express and observe each other's emotions.

Outcome:

Children strengthen empathy by understanding others' emotional expressions, develop focus by mirroring closely, and build cooperation through partner work.

9.5 Flash Card Expressions

Objective:
To enhance quick thinking, creativity, and the ability to translate emotions into movement.

Procedure:

- Prepare flashcards displaying emotions like "joyful," "nervous," "angry," and "peaceful."

- Show a flashcard, and children respond by creating a dance movement that expresses the emotion.

- Encourage them to think about body posture, facial expressions, and energy levels that match each feeling.

- Optionally, allow children to create their own flashcards with new emotions to expand the variety.

Outcome:
Children develop a deeper understanding of emotions, improve creative movement skills, and learn to express complex feelings through dance.

10. STORYTELLING:

0.1 Dance a Story

Objective:

To enhance creativity, narrative skills, and expressive movement by interpreting a story through dance.

Procedure:

- Choose a simple, familiar story — like "The Three Little Pigs" or "Goldilocks and the Three Bears."

- Break the story into parts (beginning, middle, end) and discuss the key events.

- Assign characters or scenes to individuals or small groups, guiding them to express each part through movement.

- Play thematic music to match the mood of the story, and have children perform the dance narrative for the class.

Outcome:

Children develop storytelling skills, expand their imagination, and learn to express narrative elements through creative movement.

10.2 Act and Move

Objective:

To build emotional expression, coordination, and collaborative skills by interpreting fairy tales through dance.

Procedure:

- Pick a popular fairy tale like "Cinderella" or "Jack and the Beanstalk."

- Discuss the emotions of the characters and how they can be expressed through body language and dance.

- Divide children into groups and assign each a scene or character to interpret through dance.

- Create a sequence where each group performs in order, forming a complete retelling of the fairy tale.

Outcome:

Children enhance their ability to express character and emotion, practice cooperative group work, and explore the connection between literature and movement.

10.3 Create a Character

Objective:

To develop creativity, self-expression, and individuality by creating and embodying an original character through dance.

Procedure:

- Ask each child to imagine a unique character — it can be an animal, a superhero, or a fantasy creature.

- Encourage them to think about their character's personality, movements, and feelings.

- Play music that suits their character, and let them showcase their interpretation through a short solo dance.

- Optionally, pair children to create duets where their characters interact.

Outcome:

Children expand their creative thinking, explore individual expression, and gain confidence by bringing their imaginative characters to life through dance.

10.4 Dance Adventure

Objective:

To foster teamwork, quick thinking, and improvisation through collaborative storytelling and movement.

Procedure:

- Begin with a setting like "a jungle," "a magical kingdom," or "an underwater world."

- Narrate a scenario or problem, like "a treasure hunt" or "escaping a storm."

- As you narrate, children improvise movements that fit the scenario. Guide them to react, collaborate, and adapt to the evolving adventure.

- Occasionally pause and ask, "What happens next?" to involve their ideas in shaping the adventure.

Outcome:

Children develop adaptability, cooperative skills, and the ability to create movement based on imaginative scenarios, enhancing their improvisational abilities.

10.5 Flash Card Plot

Objective:

To strengthen creative thinking, movement interpretation, and teamwork through plot-based dance activities.

Procedure:

- Create flashcards with key story elements like "a hero," "a villain," "a challenge," "a resolution," and "a celebration."

- Show a flashcard, and children use movement to interpret and act out the element.

- Gradually reveal more flashcards to build a complete story, encouraging group collaboration for interpretation.

- Conclude by allowing children to reflect on how their story unfolded through movement.

Outcome:

Children practice sequencing, express creativity in a group setting, and learn to interpret abstract concepts through physical movement.

References:

1. Laban, R. (1960). *The Mastery of Movement.*

2. Gilbert, A. (2006). *Creative Dance for All Ages.*

3. Cone, T., & Cone, S. (2012). *Teaching Children Dance.*

4. Giguere, M. (2015). *Dance Education in the 21st Century.*

HAPPY DANCING

The games in this book are categorized into warm-ups, icebreakers, memory games, body coordination, group coordination, space management, rhythm sense, stamina building, expression and emotions, and storytelling. Minimal props are needed, and each game has been thoughtfully designed to suit classroom settings. Let's dive into this world of dance and watch young dancers thrive! Teachers can personalize each activity to suit their preferred dance style. Additionally, teachers can create their own worksheets to adapt and expand the activities creatively.

"Dance-Arts is a form of

Mindful Self-Expression.

Own Your "Self", Carve Your "Style""

C R Lakshmi Karthik

Happy Dancing!!!